ULTIMATE GUIDE TO OVERCOME YOUR FEARS

Tips on how to discover and unleash your potentials

Butler John

Table of contents

Chapter 1: Self confidence

How to Build Self-Confidence

Preparing Yourself for Success
Self-confident individuals feel comfortable with themselves and their job. They encourage trust and create confidence in others. These are all excellent attributes to have.

But it's not always easy to be confident in yourself, especially if you're typically self-critical or if other people tear you down. Thankfully, there are things you can do to develop and maintain your self-confidence.

What Is Self-Confidence – and Why Is It Important?
Self-confidence involves faith in your judgment, talents, and abilities.] It's about

appreciating oneself and feeling worthwhile, despite any shortcomings or what others may think about you.

Self-efficacy and self-esteem are frequently used interchangeably with self-confidence. But they are slightly different.

We get a feeling of self-efficacy when we perceive ourselves as mastering skills and attaining objectives. This motivates us to assume that, if we study and work hard in a certain field, we'll succeed. It's this sort of confidence that encourages individuals to embrace challenging tasks and keep going in the face of disappointments. Self-esteem is a more broad notion that we can deal with what's going on in our life, and that we have a right to be pleased.

Also, self-esteem derives, in part, from the notion that the people around us approve of us. We may or may not be able to manage this, and if we face a lot of criticism or rejection from others, our self-esteem may quickly deteriorate unless we support it in other ways.

Confidence and Behavior
Take a look at the table below, which contrasts confident conduct with behavior that's connected with poor self-confidence. Which beliefs or behaviors do you identify in yourself?

Confident Behavior	Behavior Associated With Low Self-Confidence
Doing what you feel is right, despite mockery or criticism from others.	Letting other people's opinions guide your conduct.

Being ready to take chances and go above and beyond to improve things.	Remaining in your comfort zone, avoiding risk, and being afraid of failing
Admitting your mistakes and learning from them	putting in a lot of effort to hide errors and hope to address the issue before anybody discovers.
awaiting the praise of people for your achievements	praising your own qualities in front of as many people as you can.
cheerfully accepting accolades. "Thank you; I put a lot of effort into that prospectus. I appreciate your acknowledging my efforts."	dismissing praises without hesitation. "Oh, that prospectus was absolutely nothing. Anyone could've carried it out."

As these instances indicate, poor self-confidence may be self-destructive, and may present itself as negativity. Self-confident individuals are often more upbeat — they appreciate themselves and trust their judgment. But they also accept their errors and mistakes, and learn from them.

Why Self-Confidence Matters
Self-confidence is crucial in practically every part of our life, but many individuals struggle to obtain it. Sadly, this may become a vicious cycle: individuals who lack self-confidence are less likely to attain the achievement that might give them greater confidence.

For example, you may not be likely to finance a project that's proposed by someone who's plainly frightened, fumbling, or continuously apologizing. On the other side, you're convinced by someone who talks clearly, carries their head up, and answers questions with certainty.

Confident individuals inspire confidence in others: their audience, their co-workers, their employers, their clients, and their friends. And acquiring the confidence of others is one of the important methods to achieve. In the next sections, we'll explore how you can achieve this.

How to Appear More Confident to Others
Picture somebody you know who you think of as incredibly confident - what traits do they have that make you believe this? It's most likely one or more of these things:

the way they talk (tone, how they express their voice, words),\stheir passion and enthusiasm,\show competent or informed they are about anything.
You may express self-confidence via your conduct, your body language, and in what you say and how you say it. Projecting a

favorable image to others might enable you to boost your self-confidence. It's not merely a question of "faking it" — if you project with confidence, people are more likely to react favourably, and this good feedback will assist you to believe in yourself.

Body Language
When we feel worried, during meetings for instance, we prefer to make ourselves smaller by slouching, hunching our shoulders, and bending our heads. Simply sitting up straight might help you feel less anxious and more forceful .If you're presenting, extending your hands apart with palms slightly toward your audience displays openness and a readiness to offer ideas.

Face-to-Face Communication
People with low self-confidence typically find it challenging to create a strong first impression — whether they're meeting a client, addressing a meeting, or presenting a

presentation. You may be hesitant or uncertain of yourself, but you may take quick efforts to look more confident.

Engaging with others is crucial, so keep eye contact as you converse. This demonstrates that you're interested in what the other person is saying, and that you're taking an active role in the discussion. Don't fidget or look away as the talk proceeds, since this might make you seem distracted or worried.

Build Expert Power
You are likely to seem (and feel) confident when you know what you're talking about. With a depth of knowledge about a topic, you'll be better prepared to answer queries and speak on the spot. If you lack confidence because of a gap in your knowledge, concentrate on finding out additional information. Are there any related seminars or events you may attend? Is there a course you could take? Or maybe you could locate a mentor. See our post,

Building Expert Power , for additional insights on this.

Rebuilding Confidence at Work

Changes to the way they work and lengthy durations away from work significantly damage many people's confidence. One research indicated that over a third of those returning to the job after a year or more away report a lack of confidence in their own skills. You could struggle to make your voice heard in meetings, or feel lonely or alienated without the companionship of your coworkers when working from home, for example.

To resolve dips in confidence, first attempt to discover the origin of the issue. If you believe that there are things you can't accomplish, it makes sense to enhance your talents. Carry out a Personal SWOT Analysis to uncover your strengths and weaknesses. Then set out an action plan to improve on the areas where you're not so great.

Other people's attitudes or conduct might add to your lack of confidence. You can feel that your co-workers make unfair assumptions about you. Maybe you're being bullied or are vulnerable to microaggressions. If so, you need to call this conduct out.

You may utilize the Situation-Conduct-Impact Feedback Tool to make it obvious to the individual responsible that their behavior is damaging. If you don't feel secure talking to them, get support from your line manager. If they're part of the issue, talk to a team member, HR, or an employee support network if you have one. Workplace bullying or discrimination is never acceptable in any scenario. People with poor self-confidence frequently believe that they don't deserve to be happy, and that it's somehow appropriate for others to treat them cruelly. While the experience may seem quite genuine, the belief is surely not

Ways to Build Your Confidence

While there are short treatments to solve acute concerns with your self-confidence, gaining confidence in the long run takes making some modifications to your lifestyle and establishing comprehensive strategies. Here are three methods to achieve that:

1. Build Confident Habits

To grow and strengthen your self-esteem, seek to cultivate healthy habits — and break negative ones ! Regular exercise and a good diet may substantially enhance your physical and mental health . And studies have shown that obtaining a good night's sleep is related with higher optimism and self-esteem.

Working on your own branding might also assist. If you portray a favorable picture of your genuine self, you'll likely start to get the positive feedback that's so vital to your self-confidence.

2. Review Past Achievements

Your self-confidence will rise when you're able to declare, "I can accomplish this, and here's the proof." As part of your Personal SWOT Analysis, you'll have discovered items that you're excellent at, based on your prior successes.

List the 10 things that you're most proud of in a "achievement journal." Then use them to construct positive affirmations about what you can achieve. These comments are especially potent if you tend to undercut your confidence with negative self-talk.

3. Set Confidence-Boosting Goals

Setting and attaining objectives – and seeing how far you've gone – are crucial strategies to increase self-confidence. Use your Personal SWOT Analysis to develop objectives that play to your strengths, minimize your weaknesses, and take advantage of your chances.

When you've established the primary objectives you want to attain, identify the initial measures you need to take. Make sure that they're little steps, taking no more than an hour to finish. This will start the ball rolling and increase your confidence via the attainment of acceptable targets.

4. Stop Comparing Yourself to Others
Do you compare how you appear to others you follow on Instagram? Or maybe you compare your pay to what your buddy makes. Social comparison theory suggests that creating comparisons is normal. But it isn't likely to enhance your self-confidence. It may possibly have the reverse effect.

A 2018 research published in Personality and Individual Differences discovered a clear relationship between envy and the way we feel about ourselves.

5 Specifically, researchers discovered that when individuals compare themselves to others, they develop jealousy. And the more jealousy they have, the worse they feel about themselves. How can you establish self-confidence when you see that you are attracting comparisons? First, tell yourself that doing so isn't useful. Everyone is running their own race and life isn't a competition.

If you're feeling envy of someone else's life, it's also good to recall your own talents and triumphs. Keep a thankfulness notebook to better remember the places in life where you are fortunate. This might assist you concentrate on your own life vs concentrating on the lives of others

5. Surround Yourself With Positive People
Take a minute and think about how your pals make you feel. Do they boost you up, or do they drag you down? Are they continually

critiquing you, or do they accept you for who you are?

The individuals you spend time with may affect your ideas and attitudes about yourself, possibly more than you know. So, pay attention to how they make you feel. If you feel horrible about yourself after spending out with a certain individual, it may be time to say goodbye.

Instead, surround yourself with people who love you and want the best for you. Seek out those who are optimistic and may assist increase your confidence. Self-confidence and a good attitude go hand-in-hand.

6. Know When to Say No

While performing things you're excellent at might give your self-confidence a lift, it's as crucial to understand circumstances that can cause your confidence to sink. Maybe you discover that every time you engage in a specific hobby, you feel worse about yourself instead of better.

Saying no to things that tend to drain your self-confidence is alright. Certainly, you don't want to avoid doing anything that makes you feel uncomfortable since pain is frequently part of the personal development process. At the same time, there's nothing wrong with recognizing your limits and adhering to them.

Setting social and emotional boundaries assists you to feel safer mentally. It may also help you feel more in control. Self-confidence is, in part, feeling that you have control over your life. 16 Boundaries help develop this sensation of control. The next time someone recommends doing something that you know would reduce your self-confidence, politely reject. You don't have to forgo that activity forever either. Once you learn how to be more confident, you may feel strong enough to do it again—without harming the confidence you have in yourself.

Key Points

When you're self-confident, you trust your own judgment and talents, and have a strong feeling of self-worth and self-belief.

You may take immediate efforts to project more self-confidence and address the things that damage it. You may then extend these short-term methods into approaches to establish and sustain self-confidence in the future. Developing positive habits, analyzing prior successes, and setting yourself specific objectives can increase your self-esteem, and develop and sustain your confidence for the long run.

Chapter 2: Start a discovery trip

Almost everyone has experienced feelings of insignificance at some point. You could excel in sports but fail miserably in a science lab. You could be the center of attention with one group while being completely disregarded by another. The feeling of insignificance has more to do with how we see ourselves than with our actual worth as individuals.

FACT VERSUS FEELINGS

When others neglect us, it is simple to feel completely unimportant. When we feel isolated from the rest of the group, it is difficult to speak up and be heard. So where can you find out what you're really worth? Even if it hurts to feel unimportant, there is true worth in everyone of us. God created us in his image, and we were built for great things! Our souls are eroded by life, yet God values us much. God cared about us so much that He brought His one and only Son into our world to ease our suffering and give us a fresh start.

Have you ever given any thought to what it is that you really want from life? Maybe you've already made the initial step toward self-discovery, but you haven't found a way to go where you want to go. In the hustle and bustle of everyday life, dreams, personal ideals, abilities, and even personality qualities may not always appear to mean much. But being conscious of these traits might help you get a lot of insight into your inner self.

Certainly, daily priorities are significant. However, a life that is nothing more than a succession of repeating the same actions seldom brings much pleasure.

When you reach a crossroads in your life and wonder, "Who am I, really?" You can learn a little bit more about yourself by engaging in some self-discovery. Self-discovery may seem like a complicated, frightening idea, yet it actually merely involves:

looking at your life
identifying the gaps and taking action to fill them
There is no better time than the present to learn more about yourself, so here are some pointers to get you going.

Visualize your ideal self at first.

If you followed the advice that your parents, professors, friends, and other people gave you, your life may have gone rather well. If that's the case, it's possible that you haven't given much attention to your real self.

Many individuals end up defining themselves based on their interactions with other people or the activities they have consistently engaged in, never contemplating the idea of doing anything else.

But if you don't know what matters to you or who you want to be, you'll keep living for other people instead of for yourself. Since the goal of your trip is to learn what the entire picture is, you don't have to start off with it.

But try asking questions to yourself like:

What do I want in life?
In five years, where do I see myself? 10?
What am I sorry for?
What about myself makes me proud?
You may get started by looking at the answers to these questions. If you're having trouble, it could be helpful to reflect on a

moment when you were content and joyful and analyze what might have contributed.

Examine your interests.
Passions give life meaning and purpose and enrich and enhance it. Perhaps your desire to serve people led you to a career in medicine, but your present job in medical billing falls short of your desire to provide compassionate care. Finding the job you truly desire and learning the processes required for a career move might be part of living out your passion. Or maybe you might look into volunteering using your experience as a street medic.

Remember that hobbies don't necessarily need to be intricate or related to career objectives. Think about the daily activities you engage in when you have spare time. What makes you happy and makes you excited? Even hobbies, like a love of movies and music, might provide information. You may find methods to improve your life by taking some time to reflect on what you value and enjoy the most.

New experimentation
Perhaps you lack numerous interests to list. I understand. You may not recall what you used to appreciate if you haven't taken care of yourself much in a while. What would be a good method to start finding this out? Try something brand-new and completely unique. You can't know what you like until you try it, right? Maybe you've always been interested in the arts, but after taking a pottery class in college, you never tried anything. For programs in adult education that are free or inexpensive, check your local library or other community facilities.

If attending a class in person isn't an option, consider online lessons. Although they may not be exactly the same, they can often educate you enough to choose if you want to keep up the interest. It might sometimes seem a bit daunting to explore new activities, particularly ones you've never done before, especially if you choose the riskier possibilities. Try to imagine how pleased and successful you will feel later if you're feeling anxious. Taking safe risks may increase your self-esteem in addition to teaching you more about yourself.

Analyze your abilities
Most individuals have a special talent for something, whether it is cooking, home renovation, crafts, or any other ability. You can think about spending some time to evaluate your special talents and how you might utilize them as part of the self-discovery process. Perhaps your neighbors often approach you for gardening advice or your friends frequently ask you to arrange their parties. Why not put these abilities into practice if you can see yourself mastering them?
By putting your abilities to use, you may improve them and your confidence. Greater self-confidence will then inspire you to

continue developing these skills as well as any new ones you may discover.

What do you value most about yourself?
Your personal values, or the particular traits you consider to be most significant and valuable, may reveal a lot about who you are. These principles might serve as examples of the kind of life you wish to lead and the conduct you appreciate in others.

Values might consist of:

honesty
compassion\ loyalty
creativity\courage\intelligence

Making sure you are living out your ideals may be achieved by clarifying them. Making this part of your self-discovery journey might be incredibly beneficial if you've never taken the time to consider which principles you value the most.

Keep a diary

If you journal as a teenager, you may recall how it allowed you to process your feelings and dreams. Getting back into the practice of writing or blogging may help you reconnect with who you are and discover more about who you have become. A diary may aid in self-reflection, but it also has more useful uses. You may ask yourself questions and provide answers in your notebook, or you can go more into any of the aforementioned suggestions.

You may keep note of any recurring patterns in your life by journaling. Understanding harmful tendencies better may be a crucial step in the self-discovery journey. When you are aware of what is broken, you may start fixing it.

You don't excel at writing, do you? Absolutely nice. It might be helpful to just write down anything comes to mind. A sketchbook or other sort of art journal, if you're more artistically inclined, might also aid in the exploration of your feelings and objectives. Just put pen to paper, think about your perfect future, and then observe what emerges. Additionally, you may wish to attempt the psychotherapy method known as the "tombstone exercise." It entails putting in paper your core values and what you stand for—basically, what you want to say on your gravestone.

Consult a therapist

Therapy may provide a secure area where you can get some sympathetic advice when the journey of self-discovery seems overwhelming and you aren't sure where to begin. You don't have to exhibit mental health symptoms to gain from expert assistance. Counselors assist clients with a variety of problems, including clarifying objectives, changing careers, and dealing with identity concerns. Wanting to know more about yourself may not seem like a big enough issue to warrant counseling, but if you're anxious or unsure, therapy can definitely

Chapter 3: Fight your fears

What scares you? Learning how to overcome fears of failure can be challenging for everyone. Fortunately, all fears are learned. No one is born with fears. Fears can therefore, be unlearned by practicing self-discipline repeatedly with regard to fear until it goes away.

The most common fears that we experience, which often sabotage all hope for success, are the fear of failure, poverty, and loss of money. These fears cause people to avoid risk of any kind and to reject opportunity when it is presented to them. They are so afraid of failure that they are almost paralyzed when it comes to taking any chances at all.

There are many other fears that interfere with our happiness.

People fear the loss of love or
People fear the loss of their jobs and their financial security.
People fear embarrassment or ridicule.
People fear rejection and criticism of any kind.
People fear the loss of respect or esteem of others.
These and many other fears hold us back throughout life…

Here are a few techniques to help you overcome your fears and fuel your success:

Fear Paralyzes Action
The most common reaction in a fear situation is the attitude of, "I can't!"

This is the fear of failure that stops us from taking action. It is experienced physically, starting in the pit of your stomach.

When people are really afraid, their mouth and throat go dry, their heart starts pounding. Sometimes they breathe shallowly and their stomach churns. These are all physical manifestations of the inhibitive negative habit pattern, which we all experience from time to time.

Fear Shuts Our Brain Down
Whenever a person is in the grip of fear, he feels like a deer caught in the headlights of a car. This fear paralyzes action. It often shuts down the brain and causes the individual to revert to the "fight-or-flight" reaction.

Fear is a terrible emotion that undermines our happiness and can hold us back throughout our lives.

Visualize Yourself as Unafraid
By visualizing yourself performing with confidence and competence in an area where you are fearful, your visual image will

eventually be accepted by your subconscious mind as instructions for your performance.

Your self-image, the way you see yourself and think about yourself, is eventually altered by feeding your mind these positive mental pictures of yourself performing at your best.

Practice Acting "As If"
By using the "act as if" method, you walk, talk, and carry yourself exactly as you would if you were completely unafraid in a particular situation.

You stand up straight, smile, move quickly and confidently, and in every respect act as if you already had the courage that you desire.

Use the Law of Reversibility
The Law of Reversibility says that "If you feel a certain way, you will act in a manner consistent with that feeling."

But if you act in a manner consistent with that feeling, even if you don't feel it, the Law of Reversibility will create the feeling that is consistent with your actions This is one of the greatest breakthroughs in success psychology. You develop the courage you desire by disciplining yourself repeatedly to do the thing you fear until that fear eventually disappears—and it will.

Confront Your Fears Immediately
Your ability to confront, deal with, and act in spite of your fears is the key to happiness and success. One of the best exercises you can practice is to identify a person or situation in your life of which you are afraid and resolve to deal with that fear situation immediately. Do not allow it to make you unhappy for another minute. Resolve to confront the situation or person and put the fear behind you.

Move Toward the Fear
When you identify a fear and discipline yourself to move toward it, it grows smaller and more manageable. What's more, as your fears grow smaller, your confidence grows. Soon, your fears lose their control over you.

In contrast, when you back away from a fear-inducing situation or person, your fear grows larger and larger. Soon it dominates your thinking and feeling, preoccupies you during the day, and often keeps you awake at night.

Deal With the Fear Directly
The only way to deal with a fear is to address it head-on. Remind yourself that, "Denial" is not a river in Egypt.

The natural tendency of many people is to deny that they have a problem caused by fear of some kind. They're afraid of confronting it. In turn, it becomes a major

source of stress, unhappiness, and psychosomatic illness.
Be willing to deal with the situation or person directly.

As Shakespeare said, "Take arms against a sea of troubles, and in so doing, end them."

When you force yourself to face any fear-inducing situation in your life, your self-esteem goes up, your self-respect increases, and your sense of personal pride grows. You eventually reach the point in life where you are not afraid of anything.

Chapter 4: Deal with your temperament gap

Our human temperaments are traits and propensities that come with birth. They are a result of the first Adam's influence on our fallen nature, which we have inherited.

They were initially good, but the fall had a bad effect on them, thus our temperaments also need redemption. We need redemption not just for our spirits but also for our souls and even for the problems in our lives. While the redemption of our soul occurs instantly, the redemption of all the other facets of our humanity requires patience and active involvement.

Although people are not limited to any one temperament, one or two of the four fundamental temperaments are commonly used to identify us in our training. As Paul, the Apostle, explains in Romans 8:29, we are not meant to be slaves to our temperaments, but rather to be transformed into the likeness of Christ. Each temperament has a redeeming quality or a component that may be used in the process of redemption. This article attempts to emphasize ways to cope with strengths and weaknesses, particularly in the strong, dominant temperaments, although it is not a thorough study of temperaments.

The choleric, melancholic, sanguine, and phlegmatic temperaments are the four fundamental types.

Before we address the many temperaments, let's talk about emotional development and survival.

We should be aware that our environment of upbringing, our nature, which refers to who we are at our core, and our nurture (the way we were raised), all have a way of affecting who we become. If we are ready to work with the grace to bring about improvements, there is enough grace in Christ Jesus to make things right. When we gain the ability to deal with disagreements, inconsistencies, and uncomfortable circumstances, we put our maturity to the test. Many individuals have matured in their chronological development, but few have reached emotional maturity. A 20-year-old might possess the emotional development of a 5-year-old. It relies on the environment of upbringing, nurture, and nature. Many people who exhibit typical choleric tendencies are so strong that they can suppress their emotions and get rid of anybody and anything that doesn't agree with them out of survival instincts. They stay adamant about their "proper" beliefs and never experience emotional development, rather than being appropriately adjusted via healthy relationships with opposing viewpoints. Their determination to take their perspective as infallible and adhere to it regardless of what anybody says or does shows that they are motivated by a need to live. We all live egocentric lives where we believe our opinions are true and that others are less knowledgeable than we are. As a result, we even maintain our positions in the face of criticism. The capacity to respect others' rights to their opinions and to occasionally let them be who they are without attempting to "straighten" them out to fit our "standards" is a necessary component of emotional maturity.

Choleric: passionate, resolute, and knowledgeable in many areas. Weaknesses include frequent relationship changes (for the mostly choleric), indifference to others' feelings, and strong views. Leaders by nature, choleric may provide some of the most useful ideas. These positive traits may make individuals unaware of how others see them.

I have the following advice for a leader whose primary personality quality is choleric:

CONTROL YOUR STRENGTH AND VIEW IT FROM OTHERS' PERSPECTIVES

Be a good team player; remember that everyone has something to offer. Talk about your thoughts with others and allow them time to accept them. Never assume to know what others are thinking; you can never know what they are thinking about. Use your enthusiasm to inspire others instead of simply focusing on the task at hand; when others see you working alone, they get suspicious and assume that's how you want it. Do not try to claim credit for all the advancements achieved; rather, let other people's ideas bloom as well. While emotional choices may make you feel wonderful, rational choices will provide you with enduring peace of mind. Retrain your emotions to be controlled by sound judgment. When all options have been explored and the best selection can be made, objective decisions are made. When we can follow what Jesus commanded if we are to be His disciples: "Deny me (this includes my appearance), Take up my cross (that cross of shame separates me from the world and its trappings: success, etc.), and follow Him (I place my promotion and future in His hands as I obey Him)," then we have truly entered into freedom. Matt. 16:24–27

Some of the characteristics are universal to all temperaments, such as Choleric's preference for doing things "my way." Phlegmatic loves it "anyway" or the "easy way," sanguine likes it "the enjoyable way," and melancholic prefers it "the correct way."

Both the Choleric and the Melancholic have strong personalities and strong opinions about how things should be done. The choleric is explosive, but the melancholy has the potential to be implosive. Sanguines are intrepid and have a wild-west propensity; they always look for fun and new experiences, considering each endeavor as a brand-new adventure. The propensity to lose perspective on issues that need perspective is the weak side, and such lightness may result in a variety of negative outcomes. Phlegmatic people tend to be lethargic, unwilling to embark on new endeavors and see each new endeavor as a burden that may upend their comfortable life of ease. Phlegmatic is an introvert, whereas sanguine is an extrovert.

Reasons to Understand Your Temperament (And How Doing So Helped Me Understand Mine!)

One: Self-Love
You may accept yourself more fully and, therefore, love yourself more fully the more you understand yourself.

I've always needed some alone time to unwind. Since nobody else around me appeared to require it, my buddies and I both felt I was odd. After social interactions, I would also have a strong want to withdraw and, if I didn't know when I could obtain it, a kind of fear. I found out I was a "blue" when I exposed my disposition. And as I became more aware of what a blue requires, I realized that the retreat and downtime I felt forced to take were responses to my need for solitude and quiet. The more time has passed, the more I like my alone. Now that I know my temperament, I can better love myself and take care of my own needs by scheduling this.

2 Connections

You will be able to love your people more deeply if you can better understand them. People may love you more deeply if they have a greater understanding of you. My spouse is analytical, self-assured, and goal-oriented. He might be harsh and callous, doesn't offer many praises, and tends to know it all. I attempted to modify his undesirable behaviors before realizing that these characteristics perfectly sum up his crimson disposition. I made an effort to manipulate and coerce him into being the person I desired. In all honesty, I didn't get him or accept him for who he was. I now comprehend what he needs to prosper and feel loved as a result of my knowledge of his special temperament, and I am also able to embrace him for who he is, flaws and all. We've grown closer as we've become more familiar with each other's personalities and distinct wiring. As I was writing this today, he was going to do some errands. As he kissed me goodbye, he mentioned that I could have some space and solitude while he was gone. We both work from home a lot of the time.

3 Grace and Forgiveness
You may more readily show grace and forgive someone when you are aware of how

they are wired. My kid can wear me out. There was a period when I became frustrated and on the verge of hostility due to my weariness and lack of comprehension of her. Why does she need my undivided attention? I would frequently ask myself, "Why can't she do her own thing for five minutes?" I later discovered that it was because she was yellow. She enjoys being around people, craves attention, and is upbeat, vivacious, and eager to have fun. Knowing this has allowed me to show her grace and comprehend the motivations behind her actions. I include her in events, playdates, and social interactions. She has changed, and I truly adore what it means for our family. Better yet, I can now strike a balance between her needs and my own.

4 Peace
Your life will be more peaceful once you understand how you are wired.

The realization that I have a blue temperament has brought calm, clarity, and acceptance into my life. It has changed my life to become aware of my talents and shortcomings, learn how to satisfy my requirements, and develop new communication skills. Because of this serenity, I no longer feel like I'm always up against a wall, I can appreciate other people without feeling the need to alter them, and I have a more optimistic attitude toward life. These things have brought me pleasure, happiness, and fulfillment.

5 Habits
Better habits may be created by being aware of your disposition. I've formed some excellent habits thanks to the knowledge that I'm blue. My home is more organized now because I know it will improve my mood. Every week, I set aside time for isolation. I also set aside time for creativity, writing, and other creative expressions (and don't feel bad about it). I'm aware that I

sometimes battle with my self-esteem, so I make it a practice to choose to affirm myself and pay attention to my advantages. To keep my attention on the positive aspects and avoid dwelling on the negative, I also maintain a gratitude notebook on my phone. I've developed the practice of thinking things out carefully before responding rather than just going with my inclination or gut instinct.

Wait and decide
Each of us can stop and decide what to say and how to say it. What we decide may either strengthen or weaken someone. We can comprehend what each temperament needs to feel loved and safe by using the temperaments. We may use it to help us remember to use constructive language instead of a destructive one. Additionally, we may pick a kinder, smarter approach if we are aware of our disposition and what we prefer to do without thinking first. Every day, we all need to practice taking a moment

to think before speaking. We must never forget the impact of our words.

Chapter 5: Fight your deceptive imagination

When we simulate scenarios in our minds, we do so without really experiencing them. People may make judgments in this fashion without having previously dealt with a similar circumstance. For instance, we don't need to have worked in the legal field to imagine what it might be like to be a lawyer. Gilbert outlined four primary reasons why mental models are unreliable guides, however.

The first reason is that humans have the propensity to create wildly unrealistic simulations. According to studies, individuals are more likely to recall the most improbable results than the most typical ones since extreme situations are more remembered. Most individuals still have a phobia of the dentist although the majority of dental appointments are rather painless because they automatically recall the one time the dentist extracted a tooth. In certain circumstances, simulations will be based on improbable scenarios as that is what first comes to mind.

The ancillary aspects, which have been demonstrated to matter in predicting people's real response to an event, are often ignored in simulations and are instead reduced to their basic elements. Instead of merely envisioning the time spent in the dentist's chair, it might be beneficial to recall the time spent traveling, parking, and waiting during a dental visit.

Truncation is another feature of simulation that contributes to its unfavorable nature. People's coping mechanisms and capacity for active adaptation come into play immediately after an unpleasant or good incident, making them feel better. However, because this is not a part of the first response, individuals do not take into consideration or simulate what occurs following the incident. In this manner, when faced with rejection or other disappointment, individuals exaggerate their anguish.

Finally, although these expectations vanish once individuals are participating in the simulation, it is biased due to comparisons that people make. For instance, if someone simulates how much they would love eating potato chips after being exposed to chocolate, they will overestimate their pleasure because of the comparison.

Contrary to his forecast, the person's evaluation of his pleasure while eating the chips matches the rating of someone who does not make such a comparison because while doing so, he concentrates exclusively on the flavor of the chips in his mouth and ignores the chocolate he is not eating.

Gilbert proposed a simple solution: just ask other people how much they appreciate their trip. His research has shown that using this "surrogation" method, which involves questioning others, may reduce simulation forecasts' errors by half even when sufficient baseline knowledge is provided. He made the argument that, contrary to what most people would want to think, likes and dislikes are considerably more common among individuals.

Gilbert mimicked Winston Churchill's reaction when asked why human brains had such flawed and inaccurate simulation mechanisms: "Simulation is the poorest form of prediction apart from all the others." For what it's worth, simulations help you reach your objective more quickly than guessing at random.

Many Christians lose hope when they are unable to stop immoral behaviors. The fight against dirty ideas must first be won to have any chance of winning the war against impure behaviors, which are a byproduct of impure thoughts.

Satan wants you to think that you're the only one who is dealing with this issue and that you are unable to overcome it. These notions, however, are incorrect. We are often overcome by temptations (see I Corinthians 10:13), yet thanks to Christ, we can triumph against sin's devastating power. (See verses 22 and 8 of Romans.) Following God's plan will help you overcome impure thoughts through His grace.

Embrace the knowledge that Christ has already provided for your triumph.
On the cross, Christ has achieved our triumph. "God be blessed that even while you were serving sin, you obediently followed the form of teaching (instruction) that was given to you. Having been cleansed of sin at that point, you turned became slaves of righteousness (Romans 6:17–18).

You must, however, decide whether to accept that win. In his heart, Daniel "intended not to degrade himself" (Daniel 1:8). That choice must be made by every believer as well. If you seek the LORD your God with all of your heart and all of your soul, he will be found, according to God's promise (Deuteronomy 4:29).

You could suffer some defeats in the struggle against filthy ideas. You should be even more determined to win the fight despite these setbacks. You'll lose motivation if you think you can win the war without ever losing a battle. By exposing the underlying reason for every failure, God may atone for each setback. As you identify the underlying reasons for your immoral thoughts and deeds, pray to God for guidance and assistance.

You will never experience a temptation that is too strong for you to resist. I Corinthians 10:13 is cited.

The grace you need to resist temptation is something that God is glad to provide. (Read Hebrews 4:16)

You must pray for knowledge with faith if you want God to provide it to you. James 1:6–8 is cited.

Replace the hidden images that are currently in your mental gallery.

Secret, evil images in our brains are at the core of dirty ideas. We often "revive" these images and fixate on them under temptation. Most attempts to ignore the images go flat. But when we overlay God's images over them, we shall become free from the grip of the malicious images.

When you are tempted, consider what Christ went through for you. You should first clearly see Christ being wounded to atone for your sins. Consider how your sins nailed Him to the cross and the suffering He had to pay the price for your crimes. Gratefully celebrate His death, which set you free from defilement. (See Romans 6:6 and Isaiah 53:5)

The next set of images you should have in your head is those of biblical characters who failed in their fight against impurity: Samson with his eyes gouged out and David with a shattered family and kingdom. (See I Chronicles 22:7-8 and Judges 16:21.) Think about the terrible effects of sin.

Eliminate provisions for defeat that are disguised.
Put on the Lord Jesus Christ, and don't provide for your body to satisfy its lusts, says the Bible (Romans 13:14). Any indulgence in the body not only indicates that you anticipate failure, but it also encourages you to cave into temptation. It offers the mind enticing possibilities, arouses emotions, and then subdues the will. We are instructed not to follow the path

of the wicked, to entirely shun it, and to turn away from it in Proverbs 4:14–15. Eliminate from your life everything that Satan uses to destroy you, including immoral media, sensual music, sensual images, ungodly relationships, and sinful activities. You may prevent yourself from following the road of evil by eliminating these sources of temptation from your life.

Recognize that winning a war requires you to engage in several battles.

The Bible has many stories that serve as illustrations for the struggles we will encounter in life. (See I Cor. 10:6.) The Bible is replete with illustrations and cautions that fighting unclean thoughts requires enormous resolve. (See II Thessalonians 3:13, Matthew 26:40–41, and Proverbs 24:10) The longer it takes to completely defeat an adversary in combat, and it may not happen after only one conflict, the more entrenched they are. Be prepared for further assaults as our attacker prowls about like a roaring lion looking for prey. Refer to I Peter 5:8–9.

Keep in mind that your triumph will come from God's strength at work inside you.
Keep in mind that God's power inside you, not your might, will win this struggle. For it is God who causes you to choose and act under his good pleasure (Philippians 2:13). (Also see Zechariah 4:6) Whatever the devil may throw at us, God's strength in His people will always be stronger than his assaults.

Discover how to live in God's fear.
According to the Bible, "man withdraw from evil through the fear of the LORD" (Proverbs 16:6). Being conscious of the fact that God is always observing and evaluating every one of our words, thoughts, acts, and attitudes is one part of having a healthy fear of the Lord.

A devout Christian cannot indulge in sensuous ideas unless he momentarily denies the existence of a Holy God. You will be able to immediately reject impure ideas if you live in the fear of the Lord and therefore understand that God is examining every one of your thoughts (and He is).

Acquire skill with the Spirit's sword.
The Apostle Paul advised Christians to put on the spiritual armor that God has provided and to "be strong in the Lord, and in the strength of his might" (Ephesians 6:10). (Read Eph. 6:11–12.) The "sword of the Spirit, which is the word of God," is a part of this armor (Ephesians 6:17).

When Jesus was tempted by the devil, he answered with the Bible. Similarly to this, Christians are commanded to oppose the devil and firmly use the sword of the Spirit, which is the Bible. Proverbs 15:3, Proverbs 5:21, and Psalm 139:4 are good passages to commit to memory so that they might serve as regular reminders of God's presence and inspire you to live in the fear of the Lord. Romans 6's ideas explain Christians' triumph in Christ, and this text has assisted many people in achieving moral independence.

By remembering, reflecting on, and applying these and other Scriptures to your life, you may engrain them into your mind and heart. Speak the truth of God's Word when you are faced with temptations to help you stay victorious.

You should pray to God for a pure (clean) heart.
As King David did after his wicked behavior with Bathsheba, pray to God for a pure heart: "Create in me a clean heart, O God; and refresh a right spirit within me" (Psalm 51:10). A man or woman will exude an awareness of God's presence when they have a pure heart and a godly demeanor. This creates a barrier to security and control.

Discover the boundaries of God's curiosity.
Avoid uncontrolled curiosity. One of Satan's most successful traps is this one. God endowed us with wonderful knowledge, but He also restricted it: we are not to study the specifics of evil.

God desires for us to be "simple in evil, and wise in that which is good" (Romans 16:19). He never meant for us to learn evil by mental or experiential learning; instead, He wants us to recognize evil while being led by the Holy Spirit. (See I Cor. 2:12, 15–16.)

Become strong in the Spirit of God.
All believers struggle with immoral ideas. The Bible says that "the body lusts against the Spirit, and the Spirit against the flesh" (Galatians 5:17). You must overcome impure ideas to grow in the power of the Holy Spirit, and doing so demands a choice on your part—a choice to follow God.

"Grid up the loins of your mind... as obedient children, not fashioning yourself after the former lusts in your ignorance: But as he which hath called you is holy, so be ye holy in every manner of conversation [conduct]," is what the Bible instructs us to do (I Peter 1:13–15). In practice, this means that we must block a wide range of publications—books, magazines, television shows, websites, other forms of entertainment, and discussions—that appeal to the desire of the body from our eyes and thoughts.

Ones that entice you toward impurity should be swapped out for things that bolster your spirit. Deepen your relationship with God through praying, studying the Bible, worshiping, hanging out with godly Christians, and assimilating God's Word into your thoughts and actions. You may conquer your desire by fortifying your soul in these ways.

Don't be fooled; God is not amused; because what a man sows, he too will reap. Because a person who sows to his or her body will harvest corruption, but a person who sows to the spirit will reap eternal life. And let us not get tired in doing good things, because if we do not faint, in due season we will reap (Galatians 6:7–9).

Identify temptations as signs to turn to God. Temptations often stem from real human needs. God wants us to give Him our needs and trust Him to fulfill them in His time and His manner. Satan wants us to satiate those desires with immoral decisions. As a result, we need to implore God to use every temptation as a prompt to lead us to Him and teach us His ways. Jesus invites us to follow Him, accept His yoke, and gain knowledge from Him. Matthew 11:28–30 is cited. God may use the sword of the Spirit, which is His written Word, to demonstrate to us how to handle temptation. Referring to Ephesians 6:17 God will guide us out of temptation and "rescue us from evil" when we do this (Matthew 6:13).

Sinful urges, or temptations, may be turned into routes to spiritual strength. We shall learn some of the most important things about the Lord and His methods through these challenges.

Recognize that success is attainable.
Although we have all indulged in our fleshly lusts in the past, thanks to Christ, we can now resist temptation and walk in triumph. (Refer to Ephesians 2:1–10 and 1:17–19.) You will be able to overcome impure thoughts as you comprehend what Christ has accomplished for you, eliminate hidden barriers to victory, cultivate a fear of the Lord, grow in spiritual strength, and utilize temptations as signs to turn to God. And as you defeat filthy thinking, you will also eliminate unclean practices from your life.

Chapter 6: Unleash your potentials

Why does time seem to pass so quickly? Before we realize it, the week is over and the weekend has here. How can each and every day be made the best it can be? Every day, I want you to be able to live up to your full potential. I want you to have pleasure in each and every moment, even on the days when you unwind and recuperate.

Planning is the key to living up to your potential each and every day. You'll need to start learning if you're not an excellent planner. People who are organized and have strong time management skills often have more productive days.

So how can you fulfill your potential?

A Fixed Mentality
You can have a fixed mentality if you have unwavering self-perceived truths. A person with a fixed worldview created "their narrative" as a youngster, and it hasn't significantly altered over time. Simply because they had trouble in certain areas in school, they could think that they aren't very strong at arithmetic, public speaking, or writing.

Someone with a fixed perspective often thinks, "What an idiot, I knew I wasn't any good at that." Or you may say, "Well, it simply proved what I already knew; I won't be doing that again." A stuck mentality only serves to reinforce unfavorable beliefs and behaviors, making it more difficult to realize your maximum potential.

A mindset of growth

On the other side, a development attitude is the complete opposite. If you have a development mentality, you think everything is possible, but don't mistake this with being crazy! It has more to do with how you approach and address things.

Let's return to the subject of public speaking inability. An someone with a growth mindset will examine what went wrong and provide fixes to make it better moving forward. They may enroll in a public speaking course at their neighborhood community college or sign up for the Toastmasters club.

Whatever it is, they don't see failure as an impassable obstacle; rather, they see it as a brief detour on the way to their goal.

Let's return to the subject of public speaking inability. An someone with a growth mindset will examine what went wrong and provide fixes to make it better moving forward. They may enroll in a public speaking course at their neighborhood community college or sign up for the Toastmasters club. Whatever it is, they don't see failure as an impassable obstacle; rather, they see it as a brief detour on the way to their goal.

1. Keep the big picture in mind
How does the whole image seem to you? What objectives do you want to achieve? It's critical that you understand the broad picture if you want to live up to your potential every day.

Why do you behave in this way? Why do you go for work or return home to cook supper for your family? You can enjoy each day to the fullest when you have a sense of direction and reason in your life. You don't have to limit yourself to day-to-day living if you have the ability to perceive the larger picture in your life. Knowing your mission can help you feel inspired to live each day to the fullest:

2. Develop discipline

It's simple to go off course and accomplish little when there are so many distractions. Reaching your maximum potential requires you to maintain your attention on the tasks at hand. Put your phone on silence if you find yourself becoming sidetracked by it while working on a project. You'll not only accomplish a lot more, but you'll also stop yourself from doing things that are bad for your health. [5] You should throw away everything that prevents you from finishing a job.

The basic lesson is that even if you may want to watch the game on Saturday or stop working at 5 pm, learning the discipline to put off pleasure will help you exceed your limits and benefit from the additional effort.

Try answering these questions about yourself honestly to start realizing your potential.
What skills do I have?
What qualifications do I have for a job?
What am I skilled at doing?
What makes me unique?
Ask a close friend who knows you well and can assist you with the answers if you're the kind of person who struggles to see their own excellence.

You have to trust it once you're able to learn stuff about yourself! You must believe your own hype because, as the saying goes, if you don't believe in yourself, no one else will either. Your mentality, self-belief, and confidence play a big role in this.
To be able to believe it, trust it, take it and run with it, you must tell yourself and constantly telling yourself good tales about

who and what you are and what your greatness is.

You may believe in yourself and your skills because of your self-belief. When your mentality (your ideas and beliefs) are employed effectively and maintain a healthy belief system, you will be able to trust yourself and believe in your greatness. This is made possible by having the proper levels of confidence.

At the edge of your comfort zone, life starts. Finally, you may now bravely go forward to revel in the grandeur you've unleashed. This entails leaving your familiar surroundings, where you feel comfortable and secure, where things are predictable but where growth isn't always possible.

Using your newly-unleashed potential, you must take a brave step from where you are to a new area where you want to be in order to leave your comfort zone. As you walk outside of your comfort zone with your newly unlocked potential tucked under your arm, the following ideas and actions will assist you:

By trying new things and accepting new challenges, you can develop your potential.
Consider the benefits that you will experience if you realize all of your potential.
Consider fresh possibilities, outcomes, and outcomes. Consider what may and might not be.
You are the one who can start today by releasing your potential.

Strive to be Positive
It's crucial to keep a positive outlook if you want to live up to your potential every day. When you have a bad attitude, you begin to see your life and yourself as bad. When you have a poor self-image, how can you possible achieve your full potential? It all

depends on your point of view, how you see yourself, and your potential. You need to be optimistic if you want to be productive today. You'll be able to maintain concentrate on your daily goals if you have an optimistic mindset.

Recognize that you'll fail.
A person cannot become successful overnight. Failure occurs to everyone in life and is a fact of life. In reality, a large body of thought holds that failure is preferable than achievement.

Even though most of us would agree that success is preferable than failure, there is one thing to remember when it does: Don't let it get to you. Failure is failure, whether it be in your work, profession, company, or marriage. It doesn't represent who you are as a person. My acquaintance lost his whole fortune—more than $20 million—in a business transaction. I soon phoned him, and as I had anticipated, he was in deep depression. I simply had this to say to him:

"Never equate your value as a person with your economic wealth."

Accept Simplicity
Simplify the tasks that need to be completed before the day begins if you wish to perform to your highest ability. Getting started with your morning routine is simple. You'll be able to concentrate on achieving your maximum potential every day if you can discover various methods to save time and simplify your life.

You will often feel stressed and frustrated if your life is continuously chaotic and anything but straightforward. Make your life simpler!

Recharge

You must give yourself time to refuel if you want to perform at your best. You will soon burn out if you don't take any breaks while working all the time. Your body also needs time to recharge, so it's crucial to take care of that as well. Use several relaxation techniques and set some time for oneself.

Chapter 7: Listen more talk less

There is no denying that many leaders like talking. Great leaders, however, are aware that listening more and speaking less is one of the secrets to successful leadership. It could be time for a change if you often find yourself speaking with your direct subordinates or in meetings. Your workplace will probably become more open and productive if you buckle down and put the 80/20 rule into practice (listening 80%, talking/asking excellent questions 20%). Employees will feel more involved, productive, and invigorated since they are now encouraged to contribute more ideas and solutions than ever before.

The issue is that there are certain widespread fallacies about speaking and leadership, and for whatever reason, people have a tendency to buy into them. I've listed a handful of these beliefs below, explained why they're untrue, and provided some suggestions for avoiding them.

Myth 1
True, you may have a lot of wonderful suggestions for what works best, how to conduct business, how to solve difficulties, etc., but an effective leader encourages staff to seek inside solutions. When your employees fail to accomplish this, innumerable possibilities are lost because they fail to grow professionally, contribute creatively, feel confident in their roles, accept responsibility for their actions, and comprehend their importance to the success of the company. Try not to always provide all the answers, no matter how difficult it may be at times. Give your workers the responsibility, take a backward step, and allow them to come up with ideas and answers.

Myth 2

Really??? You're fascinating because you speak five languages, are an Olympian, and can balance on your head. A lot of talking, though? No, it just makes you seem boring. And you'll know you're a true bore if you often see individuals in meetings perpetually nodding and smiling feignedly, stumbling to speak clearly on the phone, or giving you a disoriented, deer-in-the-headlights expression while your voice is the only one being heard by everyone. Next time you're face-to-face with someone, try keeping your mouth shut completely, asking engaging questions instead, and only speaking when you genuinely have something special or significant to say.

Myth 3

Consider your words very carefully. If you speak too much, you could speak without thinking things through and just utter whatever comes to mind. Learning to talk less teaches you to carefully consider your words. Try to prepare your words before you speak by doing some advanced thinking. You could get the ability to keep certain things to yourself as a result, which would make you say less in general.

People often divulge things they'd want to keep secret by oversharing. Pause when you have anything to contribute, particularly if it is something private. It's important to keep in mind that once information has been disclosed, it can never again be made private.

Myth 4

It might be beneficial to speak less if you have a general idea of how long you have been talking. Generally speaking, you run the danger of losing the listener's attention after around 20 seconds of speaking. Tune in to the listener after this. Observe any signs that they are losing interest.

Watch your body language. If a listener becomes bored, they could fidget or look at their phone. Their eyes may start to stray as well. Try to finish it in the next 20 seconds so the speaker has a chance to talk.

Generally speaking, avoid speaking for more than 40 seconds at a time. Any more than this might annoy or wear out the listener.

Myth 5

Don't talk to impress others. People often speak excessively to impress others, particularly in professional settings. Consider if you are attempting to impress others if you find that you speak a lot.

Try to remind yourself that people will be more impressed by what you say than how much you speak if you tend to talk excessively to impress others.

Keep your self-promotion to a minimum and save it for topics where you can add something worthwhile to the discourse.